Grow Herbs for the Kitchen

Sheryl L. Felty

CONTENTS

Introduction

Herbs are the wonders of the culinary world. Most people can chop, dice, and sauté, but the real craft of cooking comes from enhancing the flavors of your ingredients. Often that means cooking with herbs. But herbs do more than flavor food; they have medicinal uses, are companion plants, bee attractors, good scents, and dye plants. The best way to learn about using herbs is to grow your own.

Freshly picked herbs have a flavor far more precious and delicate than dried herbs. Dried, homegrown herbs are pure, unprocessed, and pungently flavored. Herbs and herb products make fantastic gifts; jars of delicious dill pickles, fancy mint jellies, sage cheese, or potted chives spice up any holiday. Sachets and herbal teas are also welcome gifts.

The best part of all this is that it is easy to do. Growing herbs takes only a small space around the home or apartment. If you do not have space outdoors, herbs are good candidates for container growing. A few pots on the kitchen windowsill green up many winter meals. And a little bit of time each week is all it takes to tend herbs.

This bulletin will tell you how to grow, preserve, and use the fifteen most popular kitchen herbs. Enjoy!

Sheryl L. Felty is a writer and researcher. A trained horticulturalist, she has been growing her own herbs for many years.

Plan Ahead

The best way to get your herb garden off to a good start is to plan it out on paper. Decide which type of herb, what variety, and how many of each you want to grow. If this is your first experience with herbs, start small and increase the size of your garden later. Here are some ideas to consider:

- Locate the short, compact herbs in the front of your herb bed; the taller varieties behind them.
- Give some thought to color combinations. You may choose to have a green and gray garden or to brighten it up with purple basil and flowering annuals.
- Decide if you want to grow only perennials in one bed, or if you want to mix in annuals and biennials.
- Repeat herb varieties for symmetrical patterns, or plant to create a wild look.
- If you are fortunate enough to have an old stone walkway or a slightly sloping terrace, you can easily create a splendid herb rock garden. Space large and small rocks in a pleasing pattern. Plant herbs so they cascade over and between the rocks.
- You can plant a traditional, sixteenth century knot garden, a beautifully sculptured arrangement. Plant three or four types of compact perennial herbs close together to make a low hedge "knot." (See illustration.) Regular pruning is essential and much maintenance is required for this formal garden. Some herbs that lend themselves well to a knot garden are dwarf sage, lemon thyme, dwarf lavender, and winter savory.

Raised Bed Gardens

Permanent, raised bed gardens are practical and attractive for herb growing. Raised beds stand eight to twelve inches above ground level. They guarantee better water drainage and warmer soil for the plants growing there. There are a wide number of materials you can use to contain the bed: bricks, cement blocks, stone, railroad ties, logs, or anything else that suits your fancy.

Knot garden.

It is best to make the bed four feet wide if you can reach across it from both sides. Make it three feet wide, if you have access from one side only. Make it as long or short as your space allows.

If you have a plentiful supply of fertile, loamy garden soil, use this to fill up the beds. If your soil is not the best, mix:

- 1 part garden soil
- 1 part sand
- 1 part peat moss
- 1 part compost
- lime

and use this as your planting medium.

Plant on a raised bed garden the same as you would on ground level.

Essentials for
Growing Herbs Outdoors

Herbs will prosper in most types of good garden soil, especially a fertile, well-drained, sandy loam. Since most herbs are native to the poorer, rocky soils of the Mediterranean, they are able to make a fine showing under less than optimum conditions. However, if you are considering a long-term perennial bed, it is advisable to make your soil the best possible.

Most soils benefit from the addition of organic matter such as compost, chopped leaves, or peat moss. Organic matter improves the texture of soil, making light or sandy soil more fertile and able to hold a greater amount of water and loosening heavy or clay soil.

Most herbs require well-drained soil (the exception being some types of mint). Well-drained means that water seeps down into the soil at a fairly constant rate, so there is never a pool of standing water on the soil surface resulting in soggy roots for the herbs. Do not plant in poorly drained areas unless you plan to build raised beds.

All soils should be tested before you start growing. The information you get from your soil test will give you a clear understanding of your soil and its needs. You can buy a soil test kit and do your own; or for a minimal cost, you can send your soil off to a soil testing lab for analysis. Your local county extension service agent will help you with this.

A soil test will determine the soil pH (degree of acidity or alkalinity). A pH of 7.0 is neutral; below 7.0 is acidic; above is alkaline. Most herbs prefer a pH in the range of 6.0 to 7.5. If your soil is below 6.0, then it is too acid and you need to "sweeten" it with lime or wood ash. Apply five pounds of lime to each ten-foot by ten-foot area to raise the pH one point. Add the lime the fall before planting to give it sufficient time to work into the soil.

A soil test will also tell you what nutrients are available in your soil and what, if any, are lacking. The major nutrients a plant needs for growth are nitrogen, phosphorus, and potassium. These are the main ingredients in most chemical fertilizers. However, all plants need other essential elements for good growth. Some of these are calcium, magnesium, sulfur, and the many trace minerals. Most herbs require only small amounts of fertilizers and are sensitive to overfeeding.

The best time to fertilize herbs is in the early spring, just as they are planted or when they start to put on new growth. I prefer to use organic fertilizers like compost, alfalfa meal, bone meal, blood meal, or cottonseed meal. Well-rotted or dehydrated manures can also be used. Fresh manure contains too much ammonia and may burn plants. If the plants look as if they could use a lift later in the season — indicated by yellowing foliage and sparse growth — give them a shot of liquid fertilizer mixed with water. My preference is fish emulsion or seaweed.

You can use a complete chemical fertilizer such as 5-10-10, if you desire. Add a couple of tablespoons around each perennial shrub in the early spring. Mix it into the soil and water well to send the nutrients down to the roots.

Most perennial herb gardens benefit from a layer of mulch. Mulch is material spread on the soil surface to maintain even soil temperatures and moisture content. It also discourages weed growth, primarily because it blocks out light, which prevents weed seeds from germinating. Mulching the herb garden cuts out a large percentage of the time you would ordinarily spend watering or weeding.

Organic mulches decompose and add fiber and nutrients to the soil. There are several good mulches to use in your herb garden.

- chopped straw, leaves, or hay (do not use hay that has gone to seed)
- chopped bark
- grass clippings
- peat moss

Container Growing Indoors

So you want to grow herbs but you do not have the garden space? Or you simply cannot go through another winter without fresh herbs to liven up your meals? Do not despair. Herbs are some of the easiest plants to grow in containers. All they need is adequate light, warm temperatures, fertilizer, and humidity to thrive.

Choose herbs that you often use in cooking, or those that are hard to find in stores. It is preferable to select compact, low-growing herbs like thyme, marjoram, savory, parsley, sage, basil, or chives. You certainly would not want a six-foot angelica plant on your windowsill! Help your herbs stay bushy by pinching off the terminal ends of the shoots. (See illustration.)

Pots made out of porous materials are desirable because they allow excess water to seep through. Most herbs cannot tolerate "wet feet." That's why I prefer clay pots to the plastic ones. Whatever type of container you choose, *a drainage hole is a must.*

Use a suitable growing mixture. A sterilized potting soil mix is the best bet. Bags of soil mixtures are available in most gardening stores.

Help your plants stay bushy by pinching off the terminal ends.

Place a small piece of broken pottery or a few pebbles in the bottom of the container to keep the soil from spilling out of the drainage hole. Fill the container about halfway with the soil mix. Place the herb cutting or transplant in the pot and pack soil around it, leaving a one-inch headspace. Water well.

Herbs are sun lovers. They should receive at least five to six hours of direct sunlight a day. Grow-lights can be used if you lack sufficient natural light. A combination of warm and cool white fluorescent tubes is recommended. The lights should be laced about six inches from the tops of the plants and should shine eight to ten hours a day, if they are the only light source.

Herbs prefer day temperatures of 65 to 70°F; night temperatures about 10° cooler. Most houses tend to be dry in the winter. The more humidity you can put in the air, the better.

Let your plants dry out between waterings. Too much water has probably killed more container-grown herbs than too little. Feel the soil and be sure it is dry about an inch down. Water thoroughly so that it flows out of the drainage hole. Plants are like people — they prefer a warm bath to a cold shower!

Potted herbs thrive on small, regular doses of water-soluble fertilizer. Treat them with a *dilute* solution of liquid seaweed or fish emulsion once a week. (Halve the recommended dosage.)

Although insects and diseases are rarely a problem with garden-grown herbs, you may occasionally encounter a pest on indoor herbs. There are several common culprits.

Red spider mites. Cause a yellowish, mottled discoloration of the foliage. May be seen with a hand lens. Wash the plant with a soapy water solution.

White flies. Tiny, mothlike, white pests that suck the sap out of the leaves. They rise like a little cloud when the plant is disturbed. Wash with a soapy water solution. Pyrethrum insecticides successfully combat white flies.

Damping off. This disease is often a problem on overwatered herbs or newly started transplants. Be sure your potting mix is sterilized. Do not overwater. Thin plants to allow good air circulation.

Getting Plants Started

Many annual and biennial herbs are easily started from seed sown directly in the garden. Or you can get a jump on the growing season by starting your plants from seed indoors, then transplanting when the soil warms up. With the exception of tarragon, all the herbs mentioned in this bulletin can be propagated by seed.

Prepare the soil in the early spring, as soon as the ground warms up and is easily worked. Rake over the seed bed and break up any clumps of soil or organic matter. After you have a fine granular surface, scatter the seeds lightly on the top of the soil. Most herb seeds are very small and need only a fine covering of soil. Mist the seedbed with water and do not let it dry out until germination.

You can also expand your garden by propagating by division, layering, or cuttings. A neighbor with an established herb garden may be able to provide you with plants this way. To propagate by division, dig up a section of the roots of an established plant in the fall or early spring, separating them into smaller clumps with a shovel or small knife, and replant. Chives, mints, oregano, rosemary, sage, tarragon, and thyme lend themselves to root divisions.

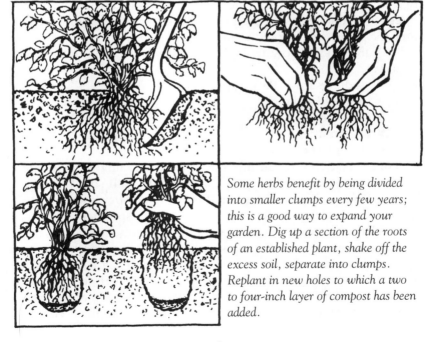

Some herbs benefit by being divided into smaller clumps every few years; this is a good way to expand your garden. Dig up a section of the roots of an established plant, shake off the excess soil, separate into clumps. Replant in new holes to which a two to four-inch layer of compost has been added.

Some herbs form roots along stems that touch the ground. These herbs can be propagated by layering. Simply mound the soil over the stem to encourage rooting. Layering is effective with mint, oregano, rosemary, sage, and thyme.

You can also propagate herbs with cuttings. Take a three-inch to four-inch shoot cut from the tip of the current season's growth. Strip all but the top two leaves from the shoot, dip the cut surface into a hormone rooting powder and plant in a loose growing medium. Once the plant is established, transplant it into the garden, if desired. This method works for marjoram, mint, oregano, rosemary, sage, tarragon, and thyme.

Transplants

Many kitchen herbs are set out from transplants or young seedlings that have been growing for eight to twelve weeks. These plants get off to a faster start and may be larger at the end of the season than the directly seeded herbs.

Space the transplants at the distance recommended on the seed package for each herb. Small herbs are usually planted eight to twelve inches apart; larger types may be separated by as much as three feet. Although the spacings may look too roomy at first, in no time the plants will fill out the area.

To successfully grow transplants you will need the following materials.

- seedlings trays, flats, or peat pots
- sterilized soil mix
- fresh seeds
- water mister
- clear plastic bags

Pour the sterilized soil mix into the flats. Gently sprinkle the seeds on the surface of the soil. Cover lightly with soil. With the mister, dampen the top of the soil. Put the flats into plastic bags to create a miniature greenhouse. (This promotes speedier germination.) Place the covered flats in a warm location (about 70°F) and check on them every few days until you notice small sprouts appearing. Remove the flats from the bags and place them in a sunny window or under grow-lights. Thin out the herb seedlings to stand two or three inches apart. Dense populations are plagued by a lack of aeration and potential disease problems. Once the herbs are larger, you may wish to transplant them into separate or roomier containers to encourage strong root and leaf development.

Before you set your transplants out in the garden, harden them off so they are accustomed to outdoor living.

- Cut back on the ration of water and fertilizer about ten days before you plan to transplant.
- Set the plants outside for a few hours on a warm, sunny day. Place them in a sheltered location so they will not be windblown.
- Gradually build up the time they are left outside each successive day, until you finally leave them out day and night.

Good Scents

The fragrance of many aromatic herbs can spice up and perfume your daily existence. Aromatic herbs can scent bathing waters, soaps, powders, oils, sachets, and potpourris. Here are a few ideas.

- *Breath fresheners.* Chew on a sprig of mint.
- *Herbal bathing waters.* Angelica, mint, rosemary, thyme. Add the herbs directly to the water or place them in a small piece of cheesecloth. Use very hot water and let the herbs steep for ten minutes. Hop in and enjoy.
- *Sachets and potpourris.* Mints, thyme, rosemary, sage, dill, savory. Combine the herbs and let them sit in a closed container for the scents to marry.

For sachets: Grind the herbs into powder and place in a small fabric bag or pillow. Place in drawers for fragrance.

For potpourris: Place the herbal mixture in an open-topped container to scent the room.

- *Catnip mice.* Crush freshly dried catnip and sew into little pillows or merry mice. A feline favorite!

Varieties of Herbs

There are hundreds of varieties of herbs to grow and enjoy, but only about fifteen varieties are regularly used in most kitchens. Do experiment with as many different varieties as you can (and Betty Jacob's *Growing and Using Herbs Successfully*, Storey Publishing, is a good book to consult for more information about additional varieties). But if you want to start small, consider planting the herbs described here.

Angelica

Angelica
(*Angelica archangelica*)

Angelica archangelica

Angelica blooms in its native Lapland on the eighth of May, the feast day of Michael the Archangel. Legend has it that the angel proclaimed angelica a cure for the plague.

Angelica is considered a biennial because it usually flowers, goes to seed, and dies in its second year. However, it sometimes takes three or four years to flower, making it the exception to the biennial rule.

Angelica prefers rich, moist soil in a partially shady location. Be sure to plant it in the back of the garden as it often reaches five or six feet in height.

The plant is majestic, with large, light green, serrated-edged leaves and thick, hollow stalks. Early in the summer, angelica blossoms with huge clusters of white flowers.

Propagate by fresh, viable seed. Once a planting is established, it will reseed itself. Harvest the leaves and stems early in the season while they are still tender and colorful.

Angelica is an aromatic used to flavor liqueurs and wines. The candied stems decorate many fancy pastries. The tips and stalks may be cooked with tart fruit to impart a natural sweetness.

Basil

Ocimum basilicum

In its native India, basil is a sacred plant, and its culture suppos-edly bring happiness to the household. In Italy, a gift bouquet of basil is a sign of romance.

Basil is a tender annual, very sensitive to frost. It is easily propagated by seed sown di-rectly in the garden after the soil has warmed up. Basil likes a soil rich in organic matter and thrives on an extra dose of compost. Plant it in full sun and be sure to water it weekly in dry weather.

Basil, Sweet
(Ocimum basilicum)

This fast-growing plant reaches about two feet in height and has large, egg-shaped leaves that curl inward. In mid-summer, small spikes of white flowers shoot up from each stalk. Pinching out the blooms, or the tips of each stem before they flower, will make the plant bushy. The leaves can be harvested throughout the summer from the growing plant.

There is a "Dark Opal," or purple, variety of basil that beauti-fully offsets the greens and the grays of the kitchen herb garden. It also imparts a rich magenta color to white vinegar.

Basil has a pungent flavor that superbly complements all types of tomato dishes. Pesto, a green sauce served on pasta, is made from ground basil leaves, garlic, olive oil, nuts, and cheese.

To dry basil, harvest just before it blooms. Hang, screen dry, or freeze.

Catnip

Catnip
(*Nepeta cataria*)

Nepeta cataria

A member of the mint family, this herb is a feline favorite. Cats love to roll in it, rub on it, chew it, play with it, and otherwise hamper the growth of your patch. But to watch them frolic is sheer delight!

The plant is a hardy perennial growing about two to three feet tall. Fragrant, velvety, gray green, heart-shaped leaves on squarish stems are characteristic of the plant. Pink flowers bloom off the terminal ends of the shoots from midsummer on. If you keep the flowers pinched off, the plants will be bushier.

Propagate by seed or root divisions.

Cut catnip just before the flowers open and hang to dry. Store in airtight containers to preserve the volatile oils. Sew little cloth pillows or fancy mice and stuff with the crushed herb. These make wonderful gifts.

Chives

Chives
(*Allium schoenoprasum*)

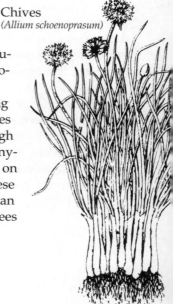

Allium schoenoprasum

Chives are native to the East, and for centuries they were used to ward off evil and promote psychic powers.

The plant is a hardy perennial, reaching twelve to eighteen inches in height. The leaves — dark green, hollow spears — poke up through the soil in the early spring, almost before anything else. Mauve blue flower balls bloom on hard, green tendrils from midsummer on. These should be cut to keep the plant growing but can be left later in the season to keep foraging bees happy.

Chives prefer full sun, rich soil, and plentiful water. Mulching around the plants is helpful to keep competitive weeds and grasses at bay.

Propagate by seeds or root divisions. A small plant will quickly enlarge and should be divided every three or four years to keep the plant healthy. Simply cut through the plant with a shovel or sharp knife in the early spring, allowing at least ten small, white bulbous roots per new clump. Set the divisions ten inches apart.

Harvest chives as soon as the spears are a few inches long. Snipping out entire spears encourages tender new growth. Chives do not dry well. Freeze for winter use.

The delicate onion flavor of chives is used extensively in cooking. Chives can be added to omelettes, soups, cheeses, salads, or fish. Sour cream and chives fattens up many a baked potato.

Dill

Dill
(*Anethum graveolens*)

Anethum graveolens

Dill has been used in the culinary arts for centuries, with the famed dill pickle being the most notable product.

Dill is a hardy annual that closely resembles fennel. However, it usually develops only one round, hollow main stem per root, and the feathery branches are a bluish green. Yellow flowers bloom in clusters of showy umbels. The dill seeds are dark brown, ridged, and strongly flavored. Dill grows two to three feet tall and can be planted in groupings to keep the plants supported in windy weather.

Propagate by seed sown directly in the garden. It does best in full sun in sandy or loamy, well-drained soil that has a slightly acid pH (5.8 to 6.5). Enrich your soil with compost or well-rotted manure for best dill growth. Once you have grown dill, it will reseed in the following years.

Dill weed and dill seed are both used in cooking; the weed is mild and the seeds are pungent. Dill weed can be harvested at any time, but the volatile oils are highest just before flowering. It adds a delicate flavor to salads, vegetable casseroles, and soups. The seed heads should be cut when the majority of seeds have formed, even though some flowers may still be blooming. Whole dill heads look striking in jars of homemade pickles and flavored vinegar. Dill seeds add zest to breads, cheeses, and salad dressing. The seeds may be threshed from the heads after drying.

Fennel

Foeniculum vulgare

There are two types of fennel grown: the herb fennel, grown for its leaves and seeds, and Florence fennel, grown primarily for its bulbous leaf stalks.

Herb fennel is a hardy biennial that often becomes a perennial in favorable climates. The plant reaches three to four feet tall and has thick, shiny green, hollow stalks; feathery branches; yellow flowers that bloom on showy umbels; and sweetly flavored, ridged seeds.

Fennel prefers a rich, well-drained soil in full sun. Add lime if the pH is below 6.0. Propagate by seed in the early spring to give it sufficient time to flower and go to seed. The leaves should be harvested just before the plant flowers.

Fennel is closely related to dill and the two should not be interplanted because they may cross-pollinate, resulting in dilly fennel or fennelly dill!

Fennel
(*Foeniculum vulgare*)

Fennel is favored in all types of fish cookery and is often used to flavor sauerkraut.

Marjoram

Majorana hortensis or *Origanum majorana*

Throughout history, marjoram has symbolized sweetness, happiness, and well-being. Shakespeare called it the "herb of grace."

Marjoram is a tender perennial native to the warm Mediterranean. In colder climates, it is grown as an annual. The plant reaches eight to twelve inches in height and has short, branched, squarish stems. The small, oval leaves are grayish green and covered with a fuzzy down. Little balls or knots grow out of the leaf clusters and the end of the branches in the midsummer. From these, white or pink flowers emerge.

Marjoram thrives in a light, rich soil in full sun. It prefers a neutral pH. Since it has a shallow root system, mulching around the plant helps to retain soil moisture and keep the weeds down.

Marjoram seeds can be sown directly in the garden after the soil has warmed up. Germination is slow — usually about two weeks. Keep the seedbed moist until the plants have sprouted. Marjoram can also be started from cuttings, layering, or division. Set transplants about a foot apart.

Marjoram is highly aromatic and its flavor improves with drying. Harvest just before the flowers open.

Marjoram is traditionally used in sausages and stuffings.

Marjoram
(*Marjorana hortensis*)

Mint

Mentha species

Peppermint, spearmint, apple mint, and curly mint are but a few varieties of the fragrant mints used in gum, jelly, and liqueur.

Mints are hardy perennials often attaining three feet in height. They are notorious spreaders and will invade the surrounding garden territory if they are not confined. They prefer a moist, rich soil and will do well in full sun to partial shade.

Mint
(*Mentha* spp.)

Mint is known by its squarish stems and its tooth-edged leaves. Clusters of white or purple flowers bloom off the terminal ends of the shoots.

Propagate by seed or divisions. Older mint plantings can be divided up every four or five years. Separate the roots into foot-sized clumps with a sharp shovel. These divisions are a nice present for a gardening friend.

The leaves may be harvested and enjoyed fresh throughout the summer. To dry mint, cut the stalks just above the first set of leaves, as soon as the flower buds appear. Hang to dry for ten to fourteen days.

Mint jelly is a favorite accompaniment to lamb roasts and chops. Minted peas are a summertime treat.

Oregano

Origanum vulgare

Oregano's fame bubbles from the flavor it imparts to pizza and other Italian specialties.

Some confusion has arisen about the relationship between oregano and marjoram. They are close relatives and oregano is often called wild marjoram.

Oregano is a hardy perennial growing eighteen to thirty inches tall. The oval, grayish green, hairy leaves grow out from the nodes. White or pink flowers make their showing in the fall.

The plant does best in a well-drained, sandy loam soil. If the pH is below 6.0, add lime before you set out the plants; oregano likes a sweet soil and a plentiful supply of calcium. Oregano thrives in full sun in a location sheltered from high winds. Mulch over the plant if winters are severe.

Oregano
(Origanum vulgare)

Oregano may be propagated by seed, divisions, or cuttings. Because the seeds are slow to germinate, you will get best garden results by setting out young plants spaced fifteen inches apart.

To dry oregano, cut the stems an inch from the ground in the fall, just before the flowers open. Hang to dry.

Parsley

Petroselinum crispum

The Greeks believed that Hercules adorned himself with parsley, so it became the symbol of strength and vigor. Parsley was also associated with witchcraft and the underworld; it was never transplanted because this supposedly brought misfortune to the household.

Parsley is a hardy biennial, often grown as an annual. There are two main types of parsley: the Italian flat-leaved and the French curly.

During the first growing season, the plant develops many dark green leaves that are grouped in bunches at the end of long stems. Italian parsley leaves are flat and fernlike; French parsley leaves are tightly curled. Umbels of yellow flowers are borne on long stalks. The plant reaches twelve to eighteen inches in height.

Parsley thrives in rich soil, endowed with plentiful organic matter. It prefers full sun for optimum growth, but it will survive in partial shade.

Parsley can be planted from seed sown directly in the garden. However, since it takes three to four weeks to germinate, it is often more reliable to set out young plants. Space parsley transplants about eight to ten inches apart.

Parsley
(Petroselinum crispum)

Parsley can be picked fresh throughout the season. To preserve for winter use, cut the leaves in the fall and dry or freeze them.

Parsley is a popular kitchen herb, found with the fanciest steak or the most common stew. It is a rich source of many vitamins and minerals, including vitamins A, B, and C: calcium; iron; and phosphorus.

Rosemary
(Rosemarinus officinalis)

Rosemary

Rosmarinus officinalis

Rosemary has been called the "herb of remembrance." This title may date back to the Greens who used it to strengthen the memory. It has appeared in religious ceremonies, particularly weddings and funerals, to symbolize remembrance and fidelity.

The perennial evergreen shrub grows two to six feet high, depending on the climate. It has woody stems, bearing thin, needle-like leaves that are shiny green on the supper surface and a powdery, muted green on the under surface. Blue flowers bloom on the tips of the branches in the spring.

Rosemary is a tender plant and must be sheltered or taken indoors for the winter in northern latitudes. It thrives best in a warm climate and prefers a well-drained, alkaline soil. Apply lime or wood ashes to acid soils testing below pH 6.5.

Rosemary is usually started from cuttings or root divisions because seed germination is slow and poor. This herb is a good candidate for container growing, allowing you to move it into protected quarters for the winter.

Harvest any time for fresh use. Hang to dry for winter supply.

Rosemary is a highly aromatic herb often used to flavor meat dishes. Use only a few needles per pot as the taste is overpowering.

Sage

Salvia officinalis

Although it is a prized culinary herb today, during past centuries sage was mainly cultivated as a medicinal herb. The name *Salvia* comes from the Latin, *salvere*, meaning "to save," and it was believed that drinking a strong sage tea improved health and prolonged life. Needless to say, it was found in every herb garden.

Sage is a hardy perennial, native to the Mediterranean. It grows two feet or so in height and has velvety, textured, patterned, grayish green leaves. The stems become woody as the plant matures and should be pruned out to keep the plant producing. Lavender flower spikes bloom in the fall.

Sage can be started from seed, cuttings, or divisions. Since the plant takes a long time to mature, transplants are usually set out. Space the plants two feet apart.

Narrow-Leaf Sage
(*Salvia officinalis*)

Sage prefers a well-drained soil in full sunlight. Enrich the soil with compost before planting, and add lime if the pH is below 5.8. Water well while the plants are young.

Harvest sparingly the first season and increase your quota yearly. The leaves can be picked any time; but it is recommended that two crops a year, one in June and another in the fall, be harvested to keep the plants less woody. Hang to dry in small bunches.

The flavor of sage is recognizable in stuffings. It especially complements heavy meats and game. Its flavor may overpower lighter herbs.

Savory

Satureia hortensis (summer); *Satureia montana* (winter)

Of the two savories grown for kitchen use, the summer variety is the mild annual and the winter is the sharper-flavored perennial.

Both savories have narrow, pointed, dark green leaves that grow out of the nodes. Small branches often arise just above the leaves. Lavender or pink flowers bloom in the late summer. Winter savory grows eight to ten inches tall; summer savory is slightly taller. Since they are small plants, the savories are good for container growing.

The savories prefer a somewhat dry soil and will survive even where the land is not too fertile. For the best flavor, plant them in full sun.

Summer Savory
(Satureia hortensis)

Summer savory is planted from seed sown directly in the garden in the early spring. Winter savory is propagated by cuttings or divisions. Space both varieties twelve inches apart.

To harvest for winter use, cut the stems in the fall, just before the flowers bloom. Cut winter savory sparingly. Summer savory can be pulled out of the ground, since it will die anyway after one season. Hang to dry.

These herbs are notably associated with bean dishes, ranging from soups to casseroles. Savory is also an ingredient of *bouquet garni*.

Tarragon

Artemisia dracunculus

Tarragon has a high standing, especially in French cuisine where it lends itself to béarnaise sauce and *les fines herbes* (a French herb blend).

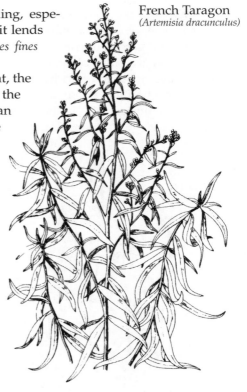

French Taragon
(Artemisia dracunculus)

Tarragon is a perennial plant, the best varieties coming from the European countries. The Russian variety is weedy and lacks the essential oils. One way to distinguish between varieties is this: the Russian tarragon produces viable seed, the European rarely does.

Tarragon grows two to three feet tall and tends to sprawl out late in the season. The long, narrow leaves, borne on upright stalks, are a shiny, dark green. Greenish or gray flowers may bloom in the fall. Since it rarely sets seed, tarragon should be propagated by cuttings or divisions.

Tarragon prospers in fertile soil with plentiful water and sunlight. It is advisable to mulch over the roots in the late fall to protect the plant from winter injury. Since tarragon becomes a rather large plant, it is often divided up every three or four years to make it easier to manage.

This herb may be harvested throughout the summer. To dry for winter use, cut the stalks a few inches from the ground in the early fall. Hang or screen dry.

Thyme

Thymus vulgaris

Native to the Mediterranean, this aromatic, perennial herb has many well-known varieties including: lemon thyme, creeping thyme, and garden or common thyme. It is a favorite plant of bees.

Thyme is a short plant, only about eight to ten inches tall. The leaves are small and narrowly oval, usually a dull grayish green. The stems become woody after a few years. Pink or violet flowers arise from the leaf axils in the early fall.

Thyme flourishes in sandy, dry soils in full sun. It is an excellent candidate for rock gardens.

Propagate thyme by seeds, divisions, or cuttings. The seeds are slow to germinate, so it is best to set out transplants. Space thyme fifteen inches apart. Older, woody plants can be rejuvenated by digging up the plant and dividing it in the early spring. Fertilize with compost or seaweed.

The leaves can be harvested for fresh use throughout the summer. To dry thyme, cut the stems just as the flowers start to open. Hang to dry in small bunches. Harvest sparingly the first year.

Thyme is one of the three essential herbs used in poultry stuffings; the other two are parsley and sage.

Thyme
(*Thymus vulgaris*)

Harvesting Herbs

The crisp days of autumn and the first frosts do not have to mean an end to cooking with herbs. Centuries ago it was discovered that herbs dry well, retaining their essential oils to enhance winter meals.

To preserve the maximum flavor and color of your homegrown herbs, harvest the herbs on a sunny day after the dew has dried from the leaves. If the herbs are dirty or have been sprayed with chemicals, it is a good idea to hose them off with a fine mist the day *before* you harvest. By not washing them after they are cut, the herbs will dry faster and you reduce the risk of losing some of the precious oils.

Pick leafy herbs just before the flowers open, when the flavor is at its peak. If the seed is to be used, allow the plants to bloom and complete their cycle. Harvest the seed heads before the seeds are scattered to the wind to produce next year's crop.

To harvest perennial herbs, cut the stems a few inches above the ground with scissors or a sharp knife. If you cut them back halfway

Bouquet Garni

The traditional French herbal mixture, bouquet garni, enhances any soup or stew it is added to. Make up little pouches in advance and have them ready to pop into the pot.

To make bouquet garni, take a four-inch square of cheesecloth and lay it flat. Pile into the middle

- 1 tablespoon parsley
- 1 teaspoon thyme
- 1 teaspoon marjoram
- 1 teaspoon summer savory
- 1 bay leaf

Gather up the corners of the cheesecloth and tie with a length of string. Store in a closed container until ready to use. (You can vary the recipe by adding rosemary, basil, celery seed, or tarragon.)

in June, you may be able to reap a second crop in the fall. Cut sparingly the first season so the plant will have adequate reserves to make it through the winter.

When harvesting annuals, I often pull up the entire plant, since it has completed its life span and will die shortly. Then I wash or gently rub the soil off the roots.

Biennials can be harvested either like perennials, cut from the stalk, or pulled from the ground like annuals.

Drying

Hang drying is the most popular method of preserving home-grown herbs. Tie the freshly picked herbs in small bunches and hang them upside down in a warm, dark, airy place. Some people place the herb bundles in paper bags with air holes punched in them to reduce their exposure to light and dust. If you have a dark, airy attic or similar room you may be successful without the bags. Try both methods and see which you prefer.

The herbs should be thoroughly dry in about two weeks or when they crumble to the touch. Do not allow them to hang indefinitely as this reduces their quality.

Strip the leaves off the stalks and crush finely if they are to be used in cooking. Tea leaves should be kept whole. Seed heads can be stored whole or threshed to separate the seeds from the chaff.

Screen drying works best with small quantities or with leaves or seed heads that have been stripped off the stem. Spread a single layer of herbs evenly over the fine mesh and place it where air can circulate freely around the entire form. The herbs should be dry in a week or two. Once they are dry, store them immediately to reduce the loss of the precious oils.

Oven drying is a highly debated topic: some people appreciate its speedy results; others denounce it because they say it vaporizes the volatile oils. If you want to give it a try, here is how it is done. Heat the oven to 150°F. Scatter the herbs on a baking sheet and put it in the oven, leaving the door ajar. Stir every few minutes. Remove the tray as soon as the herbs are crisp.

Store dried herbs in dark, airtight containers. Herbs lose their color when exposed to light. The flavor of herbs is not retained indefinitely. The volatile oils and flavor of powdered herbs perish a little quicker than that of the whole leaves.

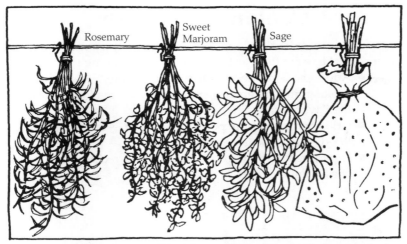

Tie freshly picked herbs in small bunches and hang them upside down to dry in a dark, airy place. Some people place the bundles in paper bags with air holes punched in them to reduce exposure to light and dust.

Freezing

Some of the thick, leafy herbs, like parsley and basil, and those that do not dry successfully, like chives, can be frozen. Frozen herbs have the same pungency as fresh, although they lack the crispness.

To freeze herbs, gently wash freshly picked herbs, if necessary. Blot dry. Strip the leaves off the stalks, chop or leave whole. Pack into bags or containers, label, and freeze.

Herbs can also be frozen in ice cubes. Simply chop the herbs, pour into an ice cube tray, pour water over them, and freeze. Pop them out of the tray and into the pot as needed.

Cooking with Herbs

If you want to cut back on your dietary salt, try using herbs as flavorings. Here are time-tested guidelines to cooking with herbs.

- Add most herbs about thirty minutes before the end of cooking time. Simmer them slowly with the food to release the flavor and retain the volatile oils.
- Dried herbs are more potent than fresh — one teaspoon dried equals one tablespoon fresh.
- Experiment with herbs! Try them in old recipes, taste new ones, combine herbs.

Hints for Drying Herbs

Don't try to pick herbs as you might daisies. Cut them. Pruning shears are fine for this. Leave four inches of stem on leafy annuals. Cut only one-third the growth of leafy perennials. In both cases this permits further growth — and further harvesting.

The delicate flavors of herbs can be spoiled by heat and faded by sun. The flowers and green leaves or herbs should be dried at very low temperatures and away from direct sunlight. Good air circulation is important in order to dry herbs quickly and thus preserve their flavor.

Dry the leaves on the stems. It's easier to strip them off when dry than when green, and it's easier to dry them on the stem.

If a commercial dehydrator, oven, or homemade dryer is used, most herbs should be dried separately in order to keep their distinct flavors from blending. This precaution is not necessary, of course, with outdoor drying.

Store large batches of herbs in several small glass jars. Small containers will retain the flavors better than large ones, which lose aroma each time the jar is opened. To keep dried herbs at their best, always keep jars tightly covered in a dry, cool, dark place. If there is no dark storage area, jars may be kept in paper bags or in a covered can or box.

Do not store herbs in a cabinet near a stove, radiator, or refrigerator. The heat from them can cause loss of flavor.

Phyllis Hobson, *Food Drying*, Garden Way Publishing.

- Use moderation. Some herbs may be overpowering if too much is used. Familiarize yourself with the strongly flavored ones — sage, rosemary, thyme, and oregano.

Herb Vinegars

Vibrant yellow and magenta vinegars add zing to a salad. A variety of herbs is used to flavor vinegars: basil (both the green and red types), fennel, tarragon, dill (both the weed and the seed heads), mints, and thyme. Most types of vinegars can be used; however, white and wine are preferable because their flavor is milder and marries better with the herbs.

To make herb vinegar, place one cup of bruised or finely chopped herbs into an old-fashioned canning jar with a glass lid. Add one or two cloves of garlic, if desired. Pour one quart of vinegar over the herbs. Cover and lace in a warm spot for two to three weeks. Taste it at that time and see if the flavor suits your fancy. If it is too weak, add more chopped herbs or allow it to set for another week or so. Strain and pour into festive bottles, adding a fresh sprig of herb to each one. Seal. Store the bottles in a cool, dark place.

It is not advisable to use metal lids, strainers, or spoons when making the vinegar because this sometimes adds an off-flavor, and vinegar will rust metal.

HERBS AND THEIR USAGE

Herb	Interplant Ideas	Culinary Suggestions	Medicinal Uses	Gifts/ Niceties
Angelica		Natural sweetener for tart fruits. Candied stems.	Digestive aid, spring tonic, bronchial problems and colds.	Fancy pastries decorated with candied stems.
Basil	Companion to tomatoes. Dislikes rue.	Tomato dishes, minestrone soup, pesto sauce for pasta, fish, zucchini casseroles.	Colds, colic, headaches, laxative.	Pesto sauce in decorative jars, purple basil vinegar, potted basil, dried herb.
Catnip	Deters flea beetles.		Upset stomachs, menstrual troubles, calms nerves.	Handmade catnip toys, fresh cuttings, tea leaves.
Chives	Companion to carrots.	Omelettes, soups, green salads, cheese, fish, vegetable dishes.	Digestive aid.	Fresh cream cheese and chive spread, container chives.
Dill	Companion to cabbage and its family members. Dislikes carrots.	Weed: salads, fish, vegetables. Seed: pickles, salad dressing, heavy meats, breads.	Insomnia, flatulence (gas).	Jars of homemade dill pickles, dill vinegar, fresh dill weed.
Fennel	Plant alone.	Salmon and oily fish, salad dressings, breads and rolls, apple pie.	Depresses the appetite, kidney and urinary problems, colic.	Freshly baked seeded rolls and breads, fennel oil.

Herb	Interplant Ideas	Culinary Suggestions	Medicinal Uses	Gifts/ Niceties
Marjoram	Throughout the garden.	Poultry seasoning, meats and game, sauces and marinades, soups, egg dishes.	Colds and congestion, colic, headaches.	Bouquet garni, sachets, tea, herb butter.
Mint	Companion to cabbage and tomatoes.	Summertime beverages, fruits, minted peas, salads, candies.	Digestive aid, colds, flu, stimulant.	Mint jelly, mint tea, candies, sachets, root divisions.
Oregano	Throughout the garden.	Pizza, spaghetti, Italian dishes, tomatoes, soups, vegetable casseroles.	Nervous headaches. Oregano oil relieves toothaches.	Dried Italian seasoning mix, container grown herbs, oil.
Parsley	Tomatoes.	Soups, stews, salads, all vegetables, steaks, fish, garnish.	Kidney stones, diuretic (promotes urine flow).	Bouquet garni, tea, fresh sprigs, potted parsley.
Rosemary	Sage, beans, broccoli, cabbage, carrots.	Meats and game, marinades and sauces, lamb, breads.	Eases nervous afflictions, strengthens the memory.	Meat marinade mix, sachet, tea, hair rinse, potted rosemary.
Sage	Rosemary, carrots, cabbage. Dislikes cucumbers.	Poultry stuffing, pork, cheeses, breads.	Headaches, tonic, digestive aid, whitens teeth.	Sage cheese, stuffing mix, tea, hair rinse.

continued

Herb	Interplant Ideas	Culinary Suggestions	Medicinal Uses	Gifts/ Niceties
Savory	Beans, onions.	All bean dishes, stuffings, fish, soups, vegetable dishes and juices.	Colds, colic, asthma. Tonic.	Bouquet garni, tea, container herb, sachets.
Tarragon	Throughout the garden.	Sauce béarnaise, fish, eggs, cold summer salads, soups, vegetable juices.	Tonic and elixir.	Flavored vinegar, tarragon jelly, *les fines herbes* mix.
Thyme	Cabbage.	Meat, chicken, fish, soups, stews, sauces, salads.	Headaches, antiseptic.	Bouquet garni, tea, sachets cuttings.

Herb Teas

To use herbs for teas, pick the leaves at the time when the volatile oils are highest. Hang or screen dry. Strip the leaves off the stems and store whole in an airtight container.

If you wish to make herb tea mixtures, experiment with proportions until you have your favorite taste. Some common kitchen herbs often made into teas are mints, sage, parsley, thyme, rosemary, marjoram, and dill.

Herb teas are usually steeped in hot water, but not boiled. Simply place one teaspoon of freshly crushed, dried herb (or one tablespoon of fresh herb) into a tea ball or strainer. Put this in the tea cup and pour boiling water over it. Allow to steep for five to seven minutes.

Herb teas can be enjoyed plain or with a little honey for added sweetness.